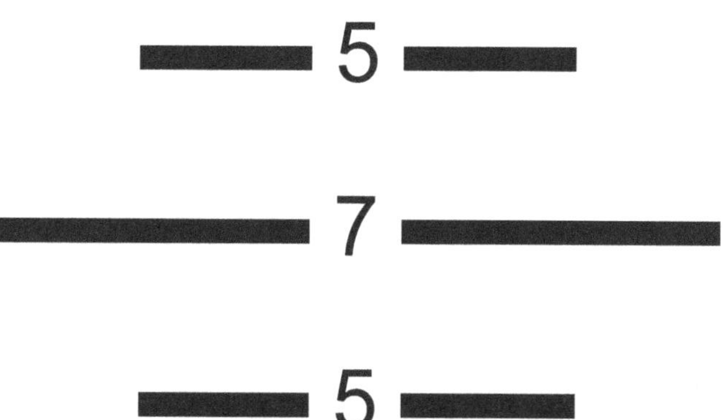

An Introspection
In Seventeen Syllables
Moments I Have Lived.

KAIKU

Author's note

A journey is never traveled alone. No matter what you might think, there is always someone in accompaniment, be it your thoughts or the actions of many others indelibly scratched in your memory.

My dynamic journey in offering 5-7-5 has been guided by two enthusiastic and incomparable individuals; Jill Scholle and Dan Klier. These two friends (of many years) have been instrumental in my efforts to bring us to where we are today. I say us because without your desire to read these Haiku passages, what purpose have I served? Life is a journey never traveled alone!

There are Toastmasters and marvelous speakers, literary giants, and Pulitzer Prize masters. I claim none of that. I claim 'brevity' and '17' syllables as my niche in literary expression. And not that it's good, it's mine!

It is the quickness of heart, the dare of the challenge, and the 'spit in your eye' mentality that "fills the cartridge of my pen." It pleases my soulful desire to offer as few words as possible and extract 10-fold of imaginative thinking.

There is a Jill and a Dan for each of you who will assist in navigating your life's exceptional experiences and place them where eyes of interest are anxiously awaiting. Join me and others: share your life as I have.

It is 'brevity'
With a style of Haiku
I share openly.

Man, you are a poet. Great Stuff!

Written by a friend
Worthy of publication
Quite the year in print.
Tim S.

Such a healing route you were able to travel as you faced these past couple years and the challenges they rang forth. Your style was creative and a very personal sharing.
M.K.

What an incredible body of work. Reading through the house like feasting on a delicious meal. You have been a busy boy in the kitchen my friend. You have mastered the art of painting large the deep places of your soul. Love that a sniper and Portuguese girl on the beach inspired you.
Scott R.

It amazes me how profound you can make 17 syllables. Do we really share the same language? You have a true talent in using poetry to express deep emotions and hold the reader's interest.
Jill S.

Raw with emotion – love and pain, regrets and hope, truth and tragedy. It touched me at points, made me choke up.
Chris S.

Will it make me blush
When I read the Kaiku book
About your lifetime.
Wendy W.

Introduction

You are holding in your hands the most unusual coffee table book. This book is a man's attempt to reveal himself in a way new and surprising to others and to himself. As Kevin shared some of his initial 'kaikus', I was given the gift of a glimpse into a side which I'd never suspected existed. As we met over several lunches, my reaction was to be absolutely blown away by the cleverness contained in three brief lines. "How long have you been writing these?" was my first question. I barely registered his answer because I was already attempting to create my own in my head and itched to dig in my purse for a scrap of paper. To my infinite amazement this was a new venue and process for Kevin. And yet, they poured out of him seemingly, effortlessly and abundantly. I'm a firm believer that new passions can be developed in one's 60's.

As I mentioned at the outset, you are holding in your hands a unique book. Pick it up off the coffee table and with your favorite beverage in hand, peruse it. Find the 'kaikus' in which you can relate. Select favorites. Allow nostalgia to wash over you. Invite someone over and debate, ponder and reflect together on this wide spectrum of emotions and insightfulness. You will share a wonderful experience drawing you closer to family and friends. You'll feel inspired to create your own 'kaikus'.

I'm still counting syllables and continue to be astounded by the wisdom, wit and perceptiveness which Kevin can pack into 17 syllables. I guarantee he'll have you picking up a pen and trying to do the same. You'll evaluate your life situations and circumstances with new eyes and context. I wish you success and the joy which accompanies artfully crafted thoughts, emotions and experiences.

Jill Scholle

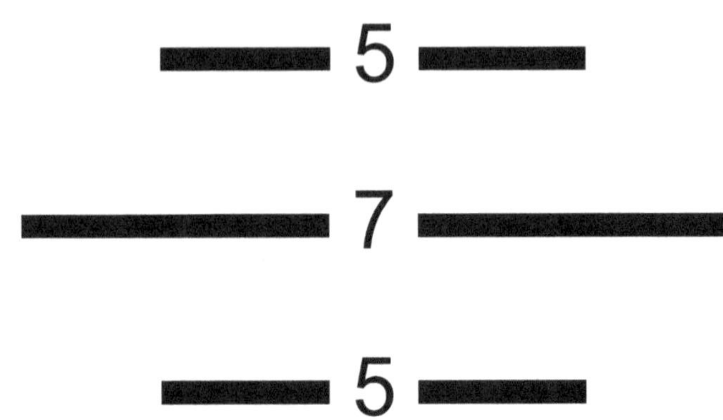

I have found it rather amazing that an existence of time can be expressed in such few words and yet provide a rather specific and definitive explanation. Of course, it could be that my introspection of time is rather simple and curt. I have found my own existence to be terribly complicated but yet ridiculously simple.

With that I leave you this thought:

I search for a word
To share life's simple journey
Syllables give voice.

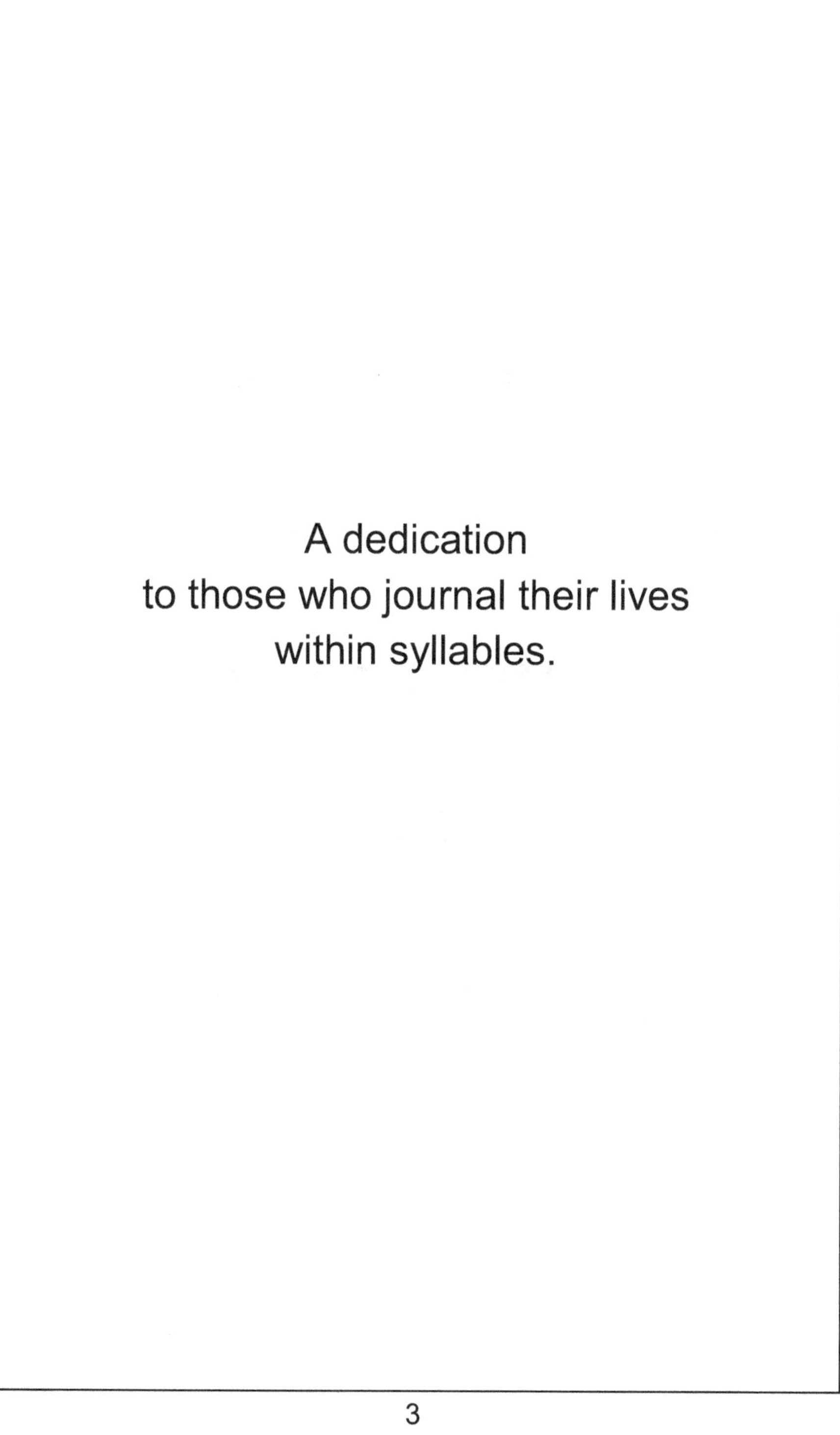

A dedication
to those who journal their lives
within syllables.

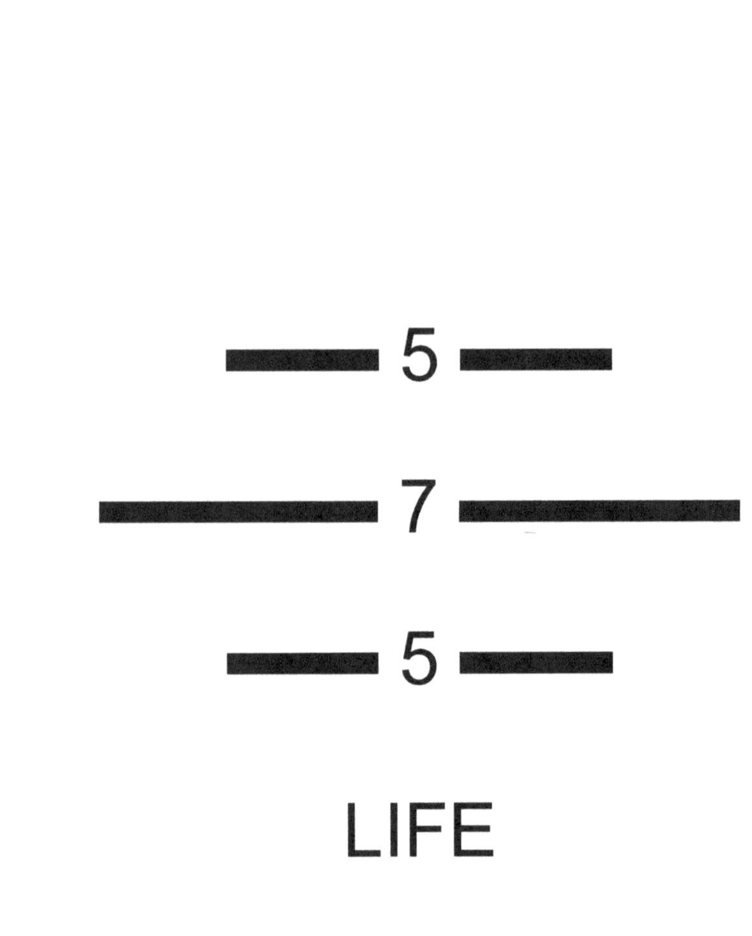

LIFE

[An essence offering great potential]

Solace in my words
A claim so easily made
Vanity or truth.

A fit black beauty
I was blind to skin color
Physique caught my eye.

I am so happy
For the precious gift of time
To be at your side.

Longing for a face
A chair at her side empty
Oh, such loneliness.

A child's artwork
Contains lines of innocence
Purely expressive.

Something now hidden
Meant everything to some
Covid mask mandate.

I just walk alone
Picturing that smile of yours
Wishing it were mine.

Slow down your actions
A lonely heart requires time
Wisdom's remedy.

A broken record
The needle has lost its groove
I miss the music.

Spirit cast downward
A challenge to find one's sight
Illness beckons one's help.

My bedside manners
A very successful man
Not for management.

Painted walls lie still
Framed paintings generate life
What is your canvas.

My pen scribes such noise
Trying to make sense of it
Silly arguments.

I saw a sadness
A man's face had lost its light
Mirror reflecting.

The eyes tell no lies
The skin is misunderstood
Smiles create friendships.

Impressions I leave
Pulling my hand from the sea
Is little I see.

A sniper for fun
Window dressing his business
Amsterdam brothel.

Irish eyes gazing
A French word being spoken
Friendships are now made.

Confident in life
Logical but challenging
Simplicity lost.

Challenges were made
Surges landing at her feet
Warrior stood strong.

Art has no language
Art is every language
Art comes from the soul.

A thorough cleansing
Left-to-right then right-to-left
Cranial washing.

A bird at cliff's edge
Has no waver in its step
Confidence of flight.

Oceans speak with strength
You must listen quite closely
God's message within.

One's gait will reveal
Is there life about each step
Walk along God's grace.

Past has slipped away
The future gives no promise
Live in the moment.

Deciding moments
Hearts answer with compassion
Logic is defied.

Hearts race with each step
Journey enjoyed hand-in-hand
Tomorrow repeats.

Blessed is one's patience
Such strength may be required
Rewards are priceless.

A man's face shows much
Is he of his word or less
Might one's eyes reveal.

Words create wonder
Let the pen ink to challenge
Puzzles will be solved.

Life's vending machine
It spirals with destiny
At the end you drop.

Wondering aloud
Does my face give it away
A smile can't conceal.

Elegance defined
Movements with purpose and grace
God's child living life.

Life should be stress free
Leave the troubles of the soul
Rejoice in friendships.

I hit with hardness
A soft touch is the right play
Three rails in the side.

Sadness is a state
With borders of loneliness
Recognition heals.

My kindred spirit
Is a person that I know
I don't think she does.

It’s just not enough
To feel one’s beating heart
It has to be heard.

One day our heart stops
Will it have been all in vain
Be remarkable.

Today I will age
Remembering a dear friend
He ages no more.

I saw a man's face
Bewildered with a blank stare
It showcased his fate.

It's the final stretch
Just ninety feet from home plate
Please take years to cross.

Does the wind whistle
If you listen close enough
It's a tune you'll like.

Reflecting today
Tomorrow has surprises
Yesterday is past.

A man sitting there
In the bright light of darkness
Moments from the end.

A sunflower's breath
Gives life to the weariest
The earth's gentle gift.

Moments to reveal
Understanding the mind's path
A brush stroke is all.

Such lessons I have learned
Life is a cruel teacher
I have studied hard.

Such a crazy laugh
A very lonely career
Not being funny.

The Olympus myth
Made gods of our great athletes
Stand pure Olympics.

They’re friends of mine
Also described as mentors
Call them Tim and Marc.

A sound so unique
Stands alone with any verse
Beauty of laughter.

More than just a weight
It causes doubt and concern
Some call it baggage.

A flame extinguished
Dusty words dousing embers
Nothing left to say.

Eyes tell a story
A smile has no language
Emotions are life.

I shall rise above
The journey and its lessons
A resurrection.

It happens yearly
It's not for the faint of heart
Will cause some panic.

Bones of any age
Move to the beat of music
Be spontaneous.

Where are you going
Blank looks beckoned this question
Following the herd.

Sing praises for life
It doesn't last very long
A lifeless void does.

Music of the heart
Gives life to the darkest soul
Please make ♪ of that.

A week together

Explore possibilities

Let’s just have some fun.

Cry for the helpless

Admire the strength of heart

Watch ‘Gone With the Wind’.

Eyes closed for seconds

A life exposed for hours.

Living eyes wide shut.

New energy found
Shoulders showing great character
A day is conquered.

A path directed
From forgings learned throughout life
Too late to turn back.

Challenges remain
An inner search continues
I seek happiness.

I am lost today
Searching for a path to take
I am blind right now.

The tears of a man
Often hidden from one's sight
Ridicule is feared.

My pen just wonders
New and past being exposed
A life uncovered.

You are a good man
I find it hard to believe
My soul is searching.

A man of many
And not always understood
Few apologies.

I cry for moments
Which had never been my way
My time has now come.

An introvert’s way
Communication method
A bicycle ride.

A flight not so long
A flight lasting forever
Anticipation.

I travel alone
Time is spent searching within
Haven’t found him yet.

We put our horns down
A fierce competitive stare
We fought another day.

As I walk, I write
Nothing is ever prepared
It's just the moment.

A smile is a smile
Really a simple gesture
It can mend the soul.

How do we exit
A life lived to the fullest
Or a wish that failed.

My glass speaks to me
Are you conquering your fears
Or being sucked dry.

Slaying the dragon
More than a knight in armor
My daily duty.

Whispers in the air
Souls searching for another
A wind blows apart.

Under the rainbow
Golden dreams are quickly born
Praise seven colors.

Walking hand in hand
A stride and stare fast and firm
Seeking winter warmth.

A child's nonsense
Grownups acting quite silly
Something to laugh at.

Holding out my hand
Three faces showed me concern
I flushed with diamonds.

Vision has narrowed
An open mind is closing
Entered politics.

Listen to yourself
Is logic behind your words
Forgive the blank stare.

Walks of innocence
Built of questions and answers
Experienced youth.

Death came upon one
Trembling without control
A vacant bedside.

Bells sounding my death
Speed and steel approaching
Superman I'm not.

Do you drink alone
An innocent opening
40 years later.

Such warmth on my face
A breeze surfing my body
Comfort so sublime.

An eye to an eye
Might be uncomfortable
Could be a new friend.

The heart will listen
One's instincts must now prevail
A weak mind suffers.

A flower misplaced
Cultivated as a weed
Careful what you plant.

Change is a constant
Change is a relinquished thought
Change is an action.

Bridging age with love
A process requiring time
Trusting one's instincts.

Shadow of a man
Either leads him or trails him
How do you stand up.

Empty victories
They meant so much at the time
No one to share with.

I listen alone
In hopes of hearing a word
Calling out my name.

Love is so fickle
We should be more like our pets
Love is just a glance.

The flight was perfect
Distance covered measured out
My first hole-in-one.

Improprobable shot

Lives are spent in search of this

I claim it ten times.

Forward I paid it

A joy ride I took for him

Leveling the field.

Stripped of character

Rising high into the sky

Palm trees without bark.

I see so little

With eyes pointing to the ground

Look skyward for life.

Required actions

An end to a beginning

Negotiation.

Success or failure

Challenges within one's means

Sensibility.

Mother's gratitude
Movement of an infant's smile
Happiness within.

Eyes of secrecy
Movements of pure elegance
A woman defined.

A kiss remembered
A darkened hall with brightness
Her smiling beacon.

Family of five

Reduced to standing of four

Picture spoke volumes.

A glimpse I shall see

Truth or a reckless spirit

I may need readers.

Righteous innocence

Searching for substantive fact

Challenging children.

Another day gone
One less heartbeat to my last
Hold me to the end.

Unexpected death
Reaching for a simpler life
A trigger finger.

Unwavering care
Conversations in silence
Man with the green thumb.

An invitation

Festival drive it became

Friendship emerging.

A man of ages

Mom's unconditional love

Dad's proudest moment.

Inspired by youth

Executed by adults

Voyage to the stars.

Bars of my despair
Preventing the great escape
A card game awaits.

Clever one you are
Mining depth within a phrase
Rewards have surfaced.

The fairness of life
Is worn like a long sleeve shirt
Tight at the collar.

5

7

5

LOVE AND FORGIVENESS

[The singular voice of love lies deaf to the heart that doesn't listen]

Can you see the wind
No darling, I just feel it
Love is like the wind.

Can't fool the ticker
Beats by its own sixth sense
Honesty's request.

My heart has been pierced
I am blinded by beauty
Powerful woman.

Her eyes captured me

Songs of her past enchanted

My heart raced freely.

Woman entering
The feeling cast was perfect
Our lives now begin.

To wake by your side
Is to greet the day with joy
Let not the day end.

Our differences
Shall not cause grief between us
If we compromise

I am such a fool
To think that love can be found
When love is not known.

Allow me my space
I must live timely moments
Without you at times.

Thinking of purpose
I now wondered where to go
She then took my hand.

A search for darkness
Blinds us in finding the light
Forgiveness is love.

A young woman's heart
Has a message for her man
Simple pleasures please.

Too little too late
The emptiness is terrible
Mirror looking back.

I met a woman
The chambers have been quiet
My heart is now heard.

A wonderful thing
A pounding heart and short breath
It's simply called love.

A white tablecloth
Eyes dazzling like jewels
Anniversary.

As I lie in bed
One pillow comforts my head
The other is you.

Just a cavity
It is built of four chambers
Such an empty heart.

Mesmerized by you
Beauty and the beast story
A happy ending.

My ache so exists
The cure lies within your heart
And your love that mends.

The countdown begins
Two lives changing forever
Some say it's Kismet.

Your ear on my chest
Reveals one's commitment
The beat of my heart.

Misunderstandings
Soulful heart beats forgiveness
Friendship continues.

The key to loving
Is vulnerability
Embrace your weakness.

A woman's beauty
Uncovered by a true heart
Happiness is blind.

Courage was given
My cover you slid under
I loved the embrace.

It's your gentle touch
That awakens the spirit
My search ends with you.

Your embrace inspires
Its strength provides joyful truth
A message of love.

When I close my eyes
Visions warm my very soul
Your smile, your presence.

A new love is found
It's rather remarkable
Christened by parents.

A day without you
Causes a heart to tremble
Let us not part ways.

A glance took my breath
My heart nervously fluttered
It happens daily.

My heart is burdened
By the lack of your once love
Another tear fell.

It was critiquing
Rather than acceptance
That kept us apart.

Light was given me
Darkness was about to fall
The truth is now clear.

I think of you now
With a heartache all my own
Your smile calms me.

I'm just a flirt
One has to give from within
In order to love.

I think back in time
When I was really happy
When she was with me.

A day in your arms
A night with breath on my chest
Moments to inspire.

Refrigerator
A blindness that robbed my soul
Of my one true love.

You are my sweet love
It's love we want to caress
Time to celebrate.

The stroke of my hand
Along her elegant back
Brings a smile to her.

To dance in her arms
Brings such joy and elation
Such warmth is unmatched.

My eyes are for you
Your movement speaks volumes
My voice sings praises.

I want to love you
With the chambers of my heart
Until they run dry.

You are a woman
I am breathless by your sight
My heart aches for you.

Such a long distance
It gets managed over time
Patience and love win.

She’s so far away

Her essence tugs at my heart

I need her near me.

I will walk alone

Looking to be at your side

Just notice me please.

There was much greatness

Little did I acknowledge

I now sleep alone

Do you really know
My capacity for love
I give that to you.

Hearts do recover
Mine will take a little time
I was unprepared.

How a woman loves
A perspective I don't know
I better find out.

I picture her walk
The grace of a young Princess
She is now my Queen.

The sun warms my face
Her actions have warmed my heart
I feel very warm.

I desire to live
With just a singular thought
To be by your side.

A white rose for her
So simple and delicate
That is who you are.

I now think of her
Lying close, feeling her breath
She is safe with me.

I've met this woman
I now see her loving me
And I love her too.

A woman's presence
Exposes man's frailties
It's okay to love.

Emptiness of heart
A terribly lonely place
Make it go away.

A Queen was just right
Too close it became a King
Single and alone.

Anticipation
The heart now struggles with doubt
Love solves everything.

On whose terms is love
If it's mine, then we shall fail
Unconditional.

Beautiful woman
Like the fragrance of flowers
So mesmerizing.

Amazing sparkle
It has remained through the years
Your eyes just for me.

How do you say love
I've known the answer for years
Calling out your name.

Simple melody
Song echoing purity
Love to hear her voice.

A resurrection
Forgiving the sins of man
Let's bear our own cross.

Time is growing short
Without you I am empty
Please call out my name.

It's so hard to breathe
When you are looking my way
Please look no further.

I cry from within
The heaviness consumes me
My heart is vacant.

Shallow happiness
A façade worn to cover
Sadness without you.

How does love escape
Without a good heart pumping
It will just go flat.

Your spirit defines
The wonderment of your soul
A reason to love.

Discipline to love
Is a simple allowance
Of giving freely.

I sleep so soundly
My dreams are potions of you
Let me never wake.

I wonder today
Is there anything to see
When looking at me.

Why did I do it

I failed to think it through

Now I dine alone.

A man I wish for

Trouble free with no worry

I had to leave her.

Sadness fills my heart

Only thy self did I care

One's true love has left.

Something remembered
A vision that simply states
I only love you.

How do you soften
The stone granite on her face
Love her endlessly.

How do I love thee
A verse I had heard before
I am left counting.

My journey starts now
Where it takes me, I'm unsure
In your arms I pray.

I am very sad
A love I so dearly miss
Tears stream down my face.

A cold fish feels warm
Ice in her veins was chilling
Our heated exit.

A picnic with you
The warm sun and soft breeze
My head in your lap.

Seconds, Minutes, Hours
There is no capture of time
That you're not with me.

The soul has such voice
The heart beats with great purpose
For you I exist.

It’s a look of love
Each time you gaze upon me
My gaze is for you.

My trembling heart
A confidence in your eyes
Will you marry me.

My eyes filled with tears
When watching your movement
Simple happiness.

Love should be simple
Doubt is what creates strain
Give your love freely.

I go to sleep now
Waiting for those dreams of you
I wake up refreshed.

I long for a love
On terms that allows freedom
I best love myself.

Eyes closed and searching
Softness being experienced
My hands touching you.

Our lives together
Really meant so much to me
A broken heart mends.

The journey goes deep
I'm falling into her soul
There is no escape.

I ask forgiveness
Only one side I belong
I ask your favor.

She offered her grace
What honor did I deserve
Her age required love.

Mend a broken heart
Great strength with needle and thread
A stitch at a time.

My haunting silence
Has only a simple cure
The sound of your voice.

Lives were fully blessed
Recognition coming late
A void now exists.

An impression made
Thirty six years of worn love
Wedding band shadow.

I reached for her hand
Her gaze said everything
I haven't let go.

A beautiful face
Da Vinci could not create
There can be just one.

A story unfolds
Just her glance turned the pages
No end was written.

A woman walks by
Enchanting fragrance is mine
Pleasure now numbs me.

Flowers expressing
A fabric canvas with strings
Draped over beauty.

It is our notebook
A love story unfolding
Our chapter begins.

Grow old without you
Is a future that burdens
My weak heart will fail.

It weakens one's knees
The mightiest always fall
It's simply her gaze.

Simple chemistry
Can create quick solutions
Lovers recognize.

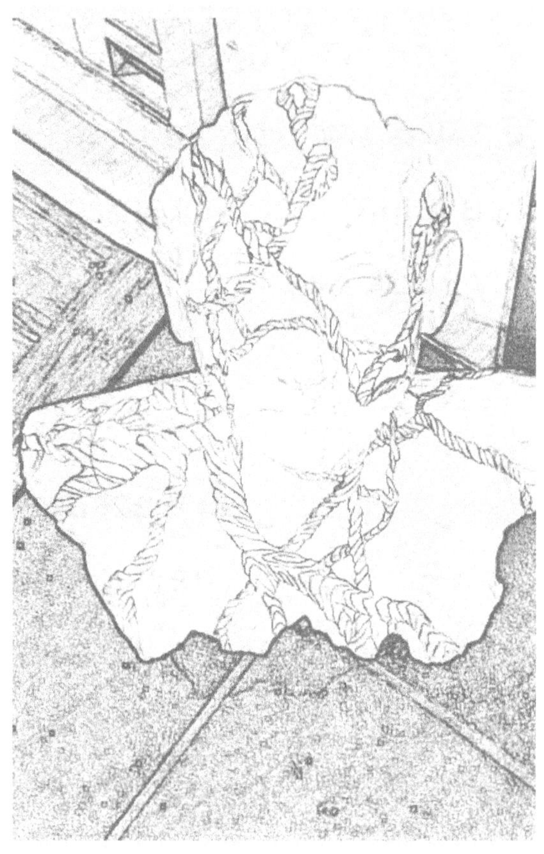

I wonder aloud

Has that voice of mine been heard

It's only my guilt.

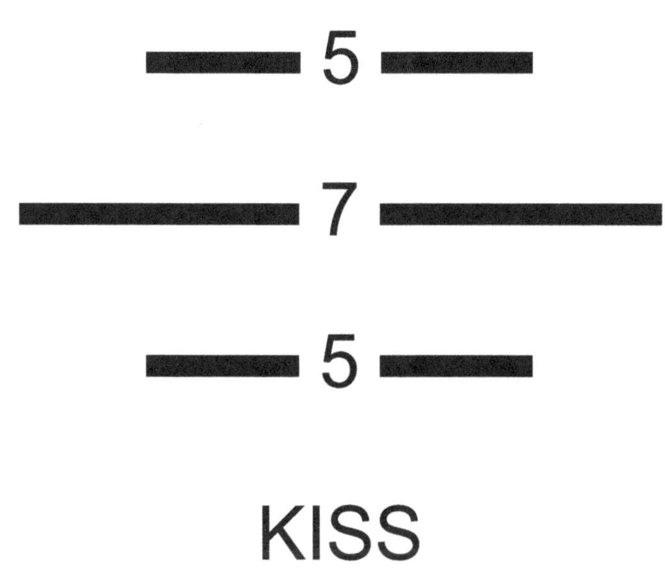

KISS

[A pleasure that ignites one's imagination]

Puddle delicious
Description of a great kiss
I enjoy daily.

Such a friend I have
I think back to where we met
A hill with a kiss.

Every smile
Forged by the shape of your lips
Brings reason to kiss.

The kiss I give you
Will be truly from the heart
It will never end.

Exquisite kisses
Seem to occupy my thoughts
My lips are starving.

I dream of your kiss
So flavorful, like a ripe peach
Let me sleep again.

It's fit for writing
Although it oozes one's lust
Just a sloppy kiss.

If you cannot kiss
Trouble in River City
No intimacy.

A kiss to wake up
A gentle softness I feel
I love the embrace.

Ever feel cotton
My kisses are much softer
They're waiting for you.

Lost in your softness
Kisses voluntarily
Embracing such warmth.

To kiss her again
Makes my mouth ache and quiver
Wondering what's next.

KISS

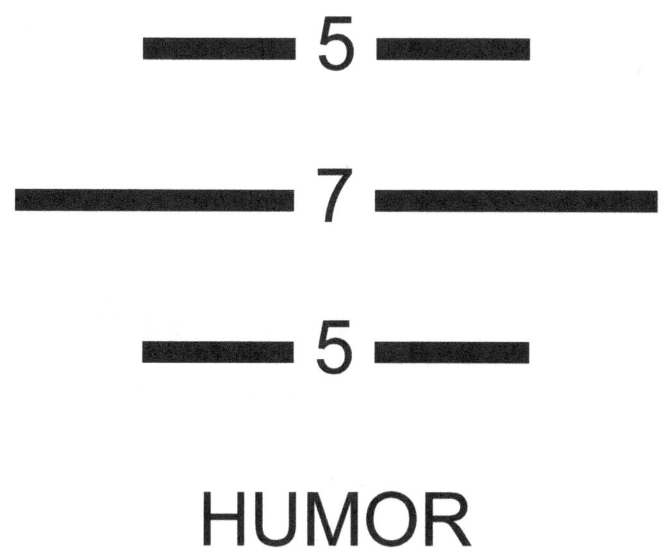

HUMOR

[To laugh is to give life to your soul]

Oh my, what to do
Yes, what to do, what to do
When I am with you.

Many necks straining
Anticipated number
One shouts out Bingo.

So silly of me
Thoughts of love embracing me
You are half my age.

Such a lovely muse

Inspiration so divine

Is she really mine.

Nails like daggers
There were ten that I counted
A woman’s two hands.

One must be steady
Or a quick wash might be yours
Number one mid-air.

Side to side we list
Up and down is the real thrill
Stomach likes neither.

How about Sponge Bob
A picture meant everything
To him, five dollars.

Pool laps are daily
Side laps have shaped over time
I should eat better.

Crypto currency
Blockchain and hidden wallets
Please don't lose your code.

Jumping tree to tree
Climbing up vertically
I'm just a squirrel.

Universally

A unifying motion

One's shoe being tied.

A garment within

Treasures held firmly in place

My entertainment.

Gyros, such delight

A true silence of the lambs

Nourishing my soul.

Bouncing towards me
How do you describe beauty
Simply stated... breasts.

Acorns drop like bombs
Squirrels scatter with delight
Winter harvest comes.

Walking on a bridge
Someone is approaching me
The water is cold.

Such sagging man breasts
Maybe it was the shadow
There was no doubt cast.

I offered my nuts
To the French and Portuguese
They loved the cashews.

It was just a strap
Kept hidden throughout the years
I loved what it held.

Ferris had it right
Dance like no one really cares
And kiss your dream girl.

A saddened spirit

Brought down by a firm red noose

Eyes reflect feeling.

A yellow magnet
Women of all ages flocked
A classic T-Bird.

Teacher in China
Poor little rich man story
My Uber driver.

Many bobbing heads
Motions like a sudden jerk
Passengers sleeping.

It pulls and it tugs
It can’t be seen, felt or smelled
It’s just gravity.

Moon slivers about
When counted there were just ten
Man’s manicured toes.

Side splitting humor
Deprecating my own truth
The reason I laugh.

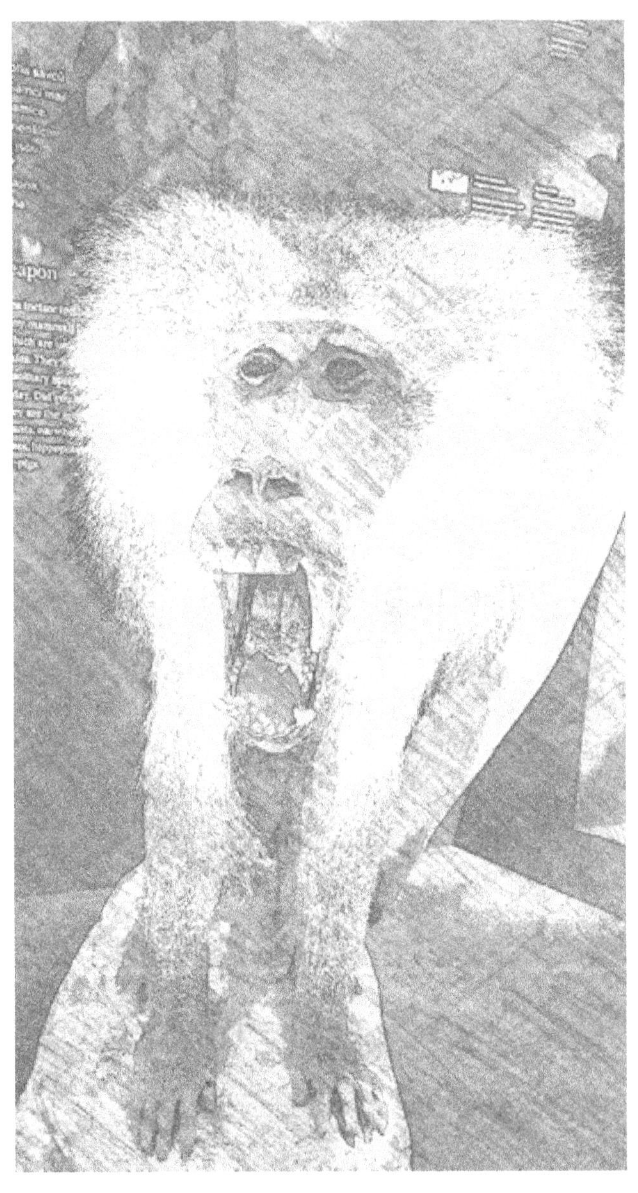

5

7

5

TRAVEL

[Lives are a journey. Let not a path go untrodden]

Flying is great fun
Layovers are a real pain
I need a shower.

Reflection of time
Actions dictate the story
A journal reveals.

I am going back
Anticipation kills me
Best not disappoint.

What a set of legs

Exposed with every step

Perfect summer dress

She was exquisite
A prima ballerina
She thanked me for that.

A train to Berlin
Six seats with comfort for two
A ride in slumber.

Motion is constant
The approach is swift and sure
It always returns.

Yellow cranes stretch high
Forms bringing life to the skies
Vienna Cityscape.

On a narrow street
A stranger approaches me
I am uncertain.

Kayaking currents
Paddling is quick and true
Destiny is found.

Language expected
Where am I going from here
Airport personnel.

My gloves were stolen
The cold requires two warm hands
Ukraine baggage search.

Eyes are upon you
You look so very foreign
You are in Ukraine.

Mystic eyes of green
Reflection of one's softness
A quick glance was mine.

Such clear eyes were hers
My path was plain and simple
Her name was Banka.

Panini at lunch
Enjoyed about Vienna
A bank loan at night.

She was persistent
Looking for a simple meal
A soft hand thanked me.

A woman's beauty
Makes one act very stupid
Ukraine dating site.

Bricks, pavers and stones
Art frescoes beneath your feet
Journeys being told.

Up, up and away

Ropes guide my short journey

Fabric kept me safe.

Movement with purpose
Strength lasting its lone journey
Delta rendezvous.

Colors of the earth
Yellow bows to skies above
Sunflowers bending.

A journey returned
Sights and voices have been felt
A man is now found.

A younger woman
Her ponytail in ginger
She gave me bus fair.

Sophisticated
Trams, subways and blue busses
Paths of Budapest.

Twenty seven years
Hiking in Slovakia
She was a doctor.

My sites beyond eyes
Offers a changing landscape
Travelling by train.

A woman's lover
A blush, a smile, a twinkle
Texting or sexting.

Steps graced with beauty
Sun creating artful shadows
Woman so divine.

Sniper sharpshooting

A challenge of great distance

Three hundred meters.

Required grouping
Three is the party of choice
Home is my circle.

Books and chocolate
A corner to find escape
Seat of happiness.

Hungary awaits
History to discover
A two-tale city.

A path never veered

Order always rules the day

Calculated end.

A chocolate gift
By a man I did not know
I have a new friend.

Countries have borders
People draw lines in the sand
Kindness mends fences.

Once a great city
Set back by communism
Rising from the ash.

We are all “criers”
Shout with great strength and fury
And stone walls will fall.

Sprechen die Deutch, Nein
Life requires no language
A German resolve.

Two for any age
Journeys enjoyed at one's speed
So "tirelessly."

Words heard in Berlin
"So afraid of the future,
Ashamed of the past."

Just like that they're gone

Swept away effortlessly

It's nature's shell game.

An almond petal
Dressed as snow in the Algarve
Brought eternal love.

White, gold, green and blue
These are the colors that make
Albufiera great.

Fashion is her love
Such beauty, grace and movement
I do admire style.

Young girls street posing
Suggestive and carefree
Simply enchanting.

Girls eating pizza
One in green and one in white
Stop yakking Czech please.

Jordan inspired
A young Czech with b-ball skills
Looking to “do it.”

Daniel was vegan
Language platforms his foray
Finding it tasteless.

The ocean captures
Soft reflections of the moon
Tides are otherwise.

A dark-haired beauty
With a captivating smile
She's from Chicago.

A fruitless escape
Crying babies next to you
An airplane's nightmare.

A bag of peanuts
She saw the look in my eyes
Alaska Airlines.

The softness of clouds
A comforter from above
I was looking down.

Lovely silhouette
A soft flowing figurine
Expressive artwork.

Road to Budapest
A carriage filled with spirits
Now comes the Danube.

A round softened stone
With a spirited message
“Travel” the world.

Budapest and Prague
A slice of old Vienna
Travels in a day.

An aisle to trek
Red roofs either side of me
Trip to Vienna.

Life in many shapes
Each in its own uniqueness
Savor difference.

Faces of many
Cultures running together
Shoulder to shoulder.

Athletic movements
Barriers of age missing
Triathlon race.

Winds have no country
Its power flows peacefully
Windmills influence.

A Shepherd alone
Searching for a single treat
Love is food for life.

Once glamorous blonde
Engaged in a quick selfie
It’s called photo bomb.

Carousel of years

Lives hop on and lives hop off

Please enjoy the ride.

Closing thoughts

If it weren't for a former boss who had the wisdom of providing me with a leather-bound book of empty pages would I have begun this journey into self-introspection.

"A single act of kindness can change the world."

That might be a little overstated, but when you think about it, it's the littlest of things that can make such a big difference. As I make that statement, I am enjoying a single M&M, plain mind you, that brings about all kinds of pleasures. From the pure taste of candied chocolate to the simple pleasure of leaning back in my chair and enjoying the moment. To think that life can be that simple. Of course, we know it isn't. That is one of the reasons I came to writing this book of Haikus. As I write on page two:

A dedication
To those who journal their lives
Within syllables.

I was once told that anyone can talk for an hour, it is the wise person who can talk for five minutes. Don't we have enough noise in our lives without the hours of conversation that are more filler than insight? Of course, there is nothing like a good story and we all have those to share. I guess my personal wish would be that everyone has that chance to share theirs. As I close the chapter on this segment of life and look forward to finding the right syllables to share my ongoing journey, I would like to leave you with a few favorites of mine. Until our paths cross again, I wish you great joy in moments that are shared within '17' syllables.

Through the looking glass
Pondered visions of success
Reflections of me.

Stories being told
Love, Sorrow and Happiness
Facial expressions.

Awful pain of heart
When one's love has little chance -
No such rekindling.

Your words are robust
Held firm and close to the vest
Says Napoleon!

Noone walks backwards
Age, health, sex or circumstance
It's forward progress.

Suddenly happens
Mystic magic tingles one
Is breeze the right word.

Nature's violins
An orchestra of crickets
Large-mouth bass delight.

Strength is tireless
Movement is without waiver
Only banks control.

A curtain of chains
A Hungarian revolt
Freedom now exists.

Is that siren mine
Are days coming to a close
Is your soul at peace.

Observing mankind
A blink and something is missed
Live with eyes open.

Such strides of purpose
A great distance was covered
Success encountered.

The genius of man
Everyone qualifies
Open minds needed.

A snowflake's journey
A destination in search
Just one enlightens.

Mannequin's spirit
Provides such sweet temptations
A dream of stillness.

Many tracks of iron
Single switch provides a path
Be the conductor.

Piano scramble
Keys of ivory dancing
The freedom of Jazz.

The jumping cholla
Pointy and well protected
A bark all its own.

Searching with blindness
Is little that I will see
Instincts must prevail.

Resolute and true
Air filled with love melodies
The language of birds.

A thought is pondered
Fresh airs whistles in my ears
New perspective found.

A sudden noise

Amuses but yet disturbs

I was heard snoring.

A man at the bar

Bike 7 was his calling

The world his claim

I am now finished

Journeys clearly revealed

A true reflection.

Marveling upward
Years of growth saw great wisdom
Standing eye-to-eye.

We celebrated
Laughter, sadness and one's love
Our relationship.

Eye's closed under warmth
Waves washing up in rhythm
Sculling in silence.

Fear acknowledgement
Requires a call to action
For the brave only.

A question I ask
Is my life's method working
It's all relative.

Ages of concern
Life's lessons are to be shared
Grandparents teaching.

People of ages
Find common threads in science
Find discourse in faith.

A wink and a smile
Living within lines of love
Make someone happy.

Immediate death
Brings life to a sudden close
Leave no stone unturned.

www.ingramcontent.com/pod-product-compliance
Lightning Source LLC
LaVergne TN
LVHW050550160826
845677LV00011B/2257

* 9 7 9 8 3 6 2 8 0 0 8 8 8 *